MIGHTY BABE RUTH

by SYD HOFF

SCHOLASTIC BOOK SERVICES
NEW YORK • TORONTO • LONDON • AUCKLAND • SYDNEY • TOKYO

ISBN 0-590-30050-4

12 11 10 9 8 7 6 5 4 3 2 3 4/8

Printed in the U.S.A. 18

For my father,
the greatest fan of all

George Herman Ruth was born in Baltimore, Maryland. His mother and father were very poor. They had to work hard to make a living, and they didn't have time to take good care of their son.

And so they sent him to live at a special school for boys in Baltimore.

All the boys at the school had to learn a trade. Young George was put right to work learning to be a tailor and shirtmaker.

But he soon showed the thing he could do best was play baseball. Even when he played against older boys, he was outstanding.

Brother Matthias, the coach of the school's baseball team, called George "a natural." He said George Herman Ruth was "born to play the game."

When George was 19 years old, he got a big break. The owner of a professional baseball team in Baltimore heard about George and came to the school to see him play.

He thought George was terrific.

"Amazing! Look at that boy pitch," he said.

"Look at him catch!"

"Look at him hit!"

"How would you like to play for our team?" the Baltimore owner asked George. "We'll give you $600 a year to start."

"You mean you'll *pay* me to play ball?" George said.

He was the happiest boy in town.

George Herman Ruth became a pitcher for the Baltimore team.

He was younger than the other players, and the coach called him "a babe."

The nickname stuck. No one called him George anymore. He was "Babe" from then on.

Soon the name Babe Ruth would become famous all over the world.

Babe Ruth did not stay with the Baltimore team for long. The owner needed money to keep the team going and he had to sell some of his best players to other clubs. Babe went to the Boston Red Sox.

Babe Ruth won game after game for the Red Sox. He was a left-handed pitcher with a blazing fastball and sharp-breaking curves.

Babe Ruth pitched 198 games for the Red Sox. He struck out 482 batters.

Most baseball pitchers are not very good hitters. But Babe Ruth was just as good at bat as he was on the mound.

When Babe hit the ball...

no one could tell...

where it would end up.

Crowds came to the ball park to see the great "hitting pitcher."

But a pitcher cannot play every day. He needs to rest his arm between games.

The fans missed Babe on the days he couldn't play. "We want a home run! We want Babe Ruth!" they would shout.

Of course, the Babe couldn't always please the fans. Sometimes he went down swinging, or was called out on strikes.

But more and more often he connected for a home run. The fans loved to see him trotting around the bases, tipping his cap to them.

Babe was a pitcher for five years. Then he decided to play in the outfield instead. As an outfielder, he could play every day and help his team win more games.

Babe Ruth pitched three World Series games for the Boston Red Sox. He won all three — and set a new World Series record. In one series he pitched 29 straight innings without giving up a run.

The record stood for more than 40 years.

Babe broke records as a pitcher. Now he set out to break records for hitting too. At that time, baseballs weren't made like they are today, and it was very hard to get a home run. But in one year Babe hit 29 home runs — more than all the other players in the American League put together.

After that every ball club in the country wished they could have Babe Ruth on their team. The wish came true for the New York Yankees. In 1920 they bought Babe from the Boston Red Sox. They had to give the Red Sox a lot of money, but they knew Babe Ruth was worth it.

The Babe went to play in New York City. The Yankees gave him a big salary. He was making more money than any ballplayer had ever made before.

Babe Ruth was famous. Fans followed him wherever he went. His picture was in every newspaper. They called him the greatest baseball player ever.

In his first year as a Yankee, Babe hit 54 home runs — a new world record. The next year he broke that record with 59 home runs.

Then, in 1927, Babe Ruth hit 60 home runs. That record was not beaten for 34 years.

But money and fame did not make Babe stuck-up. If a teammate was broke, Babe Ruth put money in his locker when nobody was looking.

If a teammate was in a batting slump, the Babe tried to help him.

Sometimes Babe would see children playing ball in a sandlot. He would give them tips and show them how to play better.

"I'd do anything for the game of baseball," he once said.

Babe Ruth loved to eat almost as much as he loved baseball. His teammates wondered where he put it all.

Babe was always ready to eat — even just before a game.

Babe Ruth ate and drank so much, he got bad stomachaches.

He also began to get fat.

"Lose some weight!" the Yankee manager told him.

So, instead of going to restaurants, Babe Ruth went to a gym.

He did exercises.

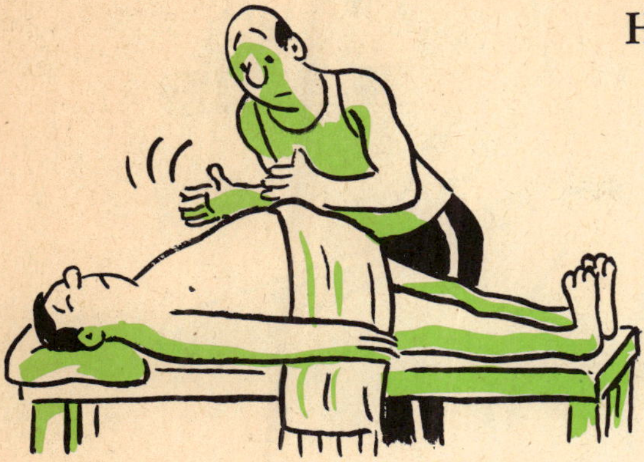

He took rubdowns.

He sat in steamrooms.

Babe Ruth lost weight. But for a time he also lost the knack of hitting a baseball.

Now the fans booed him when he came up to bat. Sometimes they even threw things at the Babe. Babe felt bad. He wanted to play well and make the fans happy.

Even when things looked bad for Babe, there were some fans who still believed in him — the children.

One day Babe Ruth got a phone call from a hospital.

"Could you come to visit the sick children?" a doctor asked. "You would make them very happy."

"I'll be right there!" said Babe Ruth.

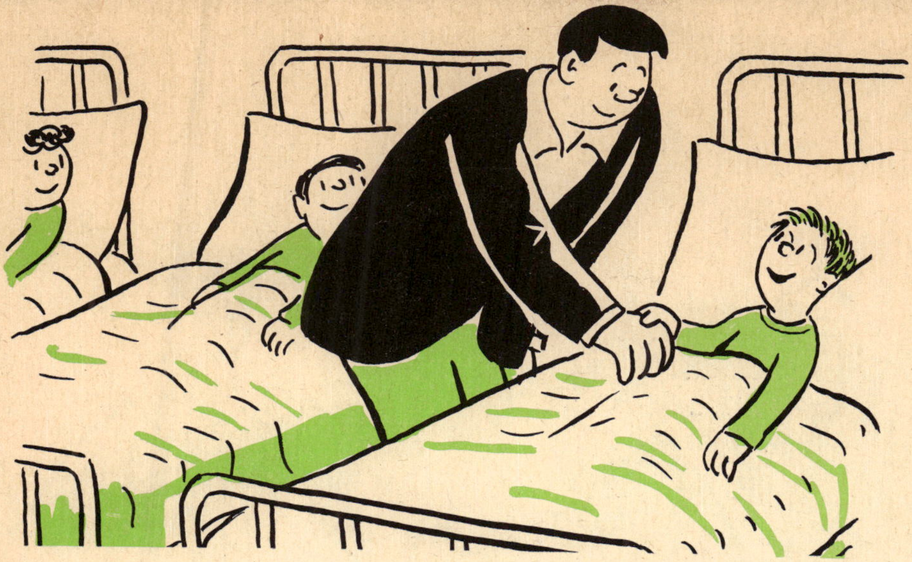

Babe Ruth shook hands with all the children. "If you hit a home run for us, we'll get better," one boy said.

At the ball park, Babe thought of the children he had just seen. "What will happen if I fail them?" he wondered.

Babe Ruth got up to bat.
He swung once and missed.

He swung a second time and missed.

The fans were booing, but the Babe didn't let it bother him. He swung at the next pitch and—CRACK! The ball was going, going...

GONE!

Babe Ruth trotted around the bases, tipping his cap in that old familiar way.

"From now on, every home run I hit will be for children sick and well," he said when he got back to the dugout.

Babe Ruth played his last game in 1935. He had played baseball for 21 years and had hit more home runs than any other person — 714 in all.

Even after he stopped playing, people kept on talking about the mighty Babe Ruth.

In 1948 the Yankees asked Babe Ruth to come for a special program at Yankee Stadium. Babe was very sick, but he got dressed in his Yankee uniform to greet his fans.

His name was called over the loudspeaker. "George . . . Herman . . . Babe Ruth!"

The people all stood up. They cheered and cheered for the greatest player in the history of the game.

3

Records are made to be broken. Babe's record of 60 home runs in one season was broken when Roger Maris, another Yankee, hit 61 home runs in 1961. And in 1974, Henry Aaron of the Atlanta Braves finished his career with 755 home runs — 41 more than the Babe.

But as long as the game of baseball is played, the name of Babe Ruth will live on forever.